I0830902

My Self-Publishing Secrets

My Self-Publishing Secrets

Lawrencia's Self-Publishing Blueprint

By: Lawrencia Lockhart

Author: Lawrencia Lockhart

Editors: Kristin Waller and Hana Whitfield

Back cover image: Kauwuane Burton

Makeup: Tasha Renee

Hairstylist: Shannoa Mullins

Stylist: Jasmon Morrow

Printed by Amazon

ISBN-13: 9798551230663

First printing edition

2020 Self-Published.

www.wrenhowsway.com

Dedication

For all the amazing people who are interested in publishing their first book, this is for you. Keep writing! Do not give up on your book. Someone is waiting to hear your story. Know that your story matters.

Table of Contents

Author's Preface

I released my first book, titled "*Things I Learned Before I Turned 31*," in 2019. When I began that project, I had no idea how to publish a book, and Google's search engine suddenly became my best friend. I started googling every question I had and utilizing all the Amazon resources that I could find. And then, 90 days later, I published a paperback book and an electronic book (eBook)!

As you can imagine, starting that course of action with no prior knowledge or experience wasn't easy. But being a determined person, I pushed on. In the process, I learned a wealth of information from the many mistakes and successes I experienced along the way. After releasing my book, I received many questions from my readers. All of them centered on one topic; how does someone publish and release a book? To help answer that question, I created this "how-to" book to assist you and other budding authors through your self-publishing journeys.

Please note: I wrote this book based on my research and my experience after I self-published for the first time. I sincerely hope that it will help you publish and release your book. Since there are multiple ways to release books, feel free to use any additional resources with which you are familiar or that you learn.

Self-publishing can turn into an expensive proposition. However, less costly self-publishing options exist and do not require you to spend an arm and a leg to publish your book.

As an author, writer, and blogger myself, I understand and applaud your passion for writing. I believe that everyone has a beautiful tale to share that may help others in some way.

So, why are you waiting? Lol. I want to help you tell your story and release your book without making my mistakes in the process.

Knowledge is power. If knowing my mistakes can give you the advantage to succeed on your journey to produce your first book, I encourage you to do it!

Book Expectations

- This book will serve as a guide of how to publish a book through *Amazon Kindle Direct Publishing (KDP)*.

- This book will provide resources for editors.

- This book is not going to tell you how to write a book. This book starts from the point of someone having his or her book manuscript ready for review.

- This book will provide you with my marketing tips I utilized and the publishing company I utilized for my book.

- This book does not guarantee you will have book sales.

- If the steps are followed, you can produce a book, and you will be welcomed into the world as an author.

- Also, be on the lookout for areas in the book labeled: *****Personal Mistake story*****, in which I share my personal mistakes, in hopes to keep you from making similar mistakes.

Now that you are finished writing your manuscript, — let's go and get this book published.

Chapter 1: The Beginning

Congratulations on completing your manuscript! You are ready for the next step in your journey to publish and release your book, and it is time to find a publisher.

So, where do you go? And who do you pick?

I published my first book with *Amazon KDP* using its tremendous resources and several outside sources.

I have included the tools that helped me the most in this book. You can also find them on *Amazon KDP* and other websites.

Why I Chose *Amazon KDP*

I chose *Amazon KDP* because it provided young authors like me, just starting our lives in a vast and competitive world, with many free resources. I discovered that I had a free ISBN, and as a Prime member, I had two free shipping days to ship my paperback books. The best part was no fees! And for me, it became a win-win situation.

I highly recommend *Amazon KDP* to other authors who want to self-publish and release their books, and I hope this book serves as a guide to your journey.

How KDP Works

To access *Amazon's Kindle Direct Publishing*, or *KDP*, click on the following link: www.amazonkdp.com. You can also do a Google search for *Amazon KDP*.

Creating a KDP Account

The first thing to do is to create an *Amazon KDP* account. Save your account and login information so that you can readily access the site.

Enter all information required for your book payments and possible royalty payouts.

At this point, you will be ready to begin processing, organizing and publishing your book.

Go Back to the KDP Home Page

The top of the page has a horizontal menu with several links. Clicking on the **Bookshelf** link will bring up publishing options. You can choose to publish a paperback or an eBook, or even both books at the same time!

For my first book, I decided to publish a paperback and an eBook.

Amazon KDP also provides its users with a unique tool to link your paperback book and eBook together and submit for publish at the same time.

Adding Text to Your Manuscript as You Set up for Self-Publication

As you write more of your story, *Amazon KDP* permits you to add newly written chapters and text in any quantity to the chapters already saved in the *KDP* server.

6

Selecting a Page Size for Your Paperback Book

To publish a paperback book, select the correct cover size for your book. *Amazon KDP* has an enormous selection of sizes from which to choose. The most common paperback sizes are 6x9 inches and 5.5x8.5 inches. For my first paperback book, I chose the 6x9 inch size.

What's Next in Chapter 2

So stay tuned! In the next chapter, we will walk through all the required fields to publish your eBook, Paperback, or both. We are one-step closer to publishing your book!

Helpful Tip: As an author who is about to self-publish a book, you will experience the joy of completing all the publication steps to make your book a reality!

Remember, if you get overwhelmed:

- Check out the helpful links mentioned at the back of this book. You will find several helpful websites and applications.

- You will find paid professionals online who are willing to assist you with every stage of publishing your book for a fee.

- And you will find a ton of free Amazon resources, videos, and guides as well.

Chapter 2: Amazon Fields

Once you click on the type of book you want to publish, several fields will appear. I divided the fields for a Kindle eBook from those that apply to a Paperback. Several fields are the same for eBooks and paperback books. Fill in the appropriate ones for the book(s) you want to publish.

The fields for an eBook are:

Kindle eBook Details

Language

Book Title

Subtitle (Optional)

Series, Series Name, and Series Number (Optional)

Edition Number (Optional)

Author Name: Primary Author or Contributor

Contributors (Optional)

(Editor, Foreword, Illustrator, Introduction, Narrator, Photographer, Preface, Translator, Contributions By)

Description

Up to 4000 characters. Take your time on this portion of your book, because others will be able to read this portion of your book to determine if they want to purchase the book or not.

Publishing Rights

Do you own the copyright or it is a public domain work?

Keywords (Optional)

The keywords help someone searching in Amazon; they are better able to locate your book. I recommend getting help on this portion of the book, because this can affect how others find your book. Fiverr is a great resource to use for someone to assist with helping you select your keywords. You are allowed to input up to seven keywords about your book.

Categories

(Fiction, Nonfiction, Juvenile Fiction, Juvenile Nonfiction, Comic and Graphic Novels, Education and Reference, Literary Collections, Non Classifiable) Within each category there are multiple sub categories. You are able to select two categories.

Age and Grade Range (Optional)

Minimum and Maximum

US Grade Range (Optional)

Minimum and Maximum

Pre-Order

<u>Personal Mistake story</u>* *I did a pre-order on my first book and pulled it back to make additional changes. If your book is complete, you can schedule a pre-order for your eBook. Amazon allows you to push your pre-order date out as much as one year before your book release date. However, I encourage you to complete your book prior to your pre-order request.*

Kindle eBook Content

Manuscript

Upload your eBook Manuscript

Digital Rights Management (DRM)

DRM allows readers to lend their eBook to someone else to read.

 Upload eBook manuscript

Kindle eBook Cover

Upload your book cover.

Kindle eBook Preview

Kindle eBook ISBN and Publisher (Optional)

Kindle eBook Pricing

KDP Select Enrollment (Optional)

Territories

All territories (worldwide rights) or Individual territories

Royalty and Pricing

Select a royalty plan. Set your Kindle eBook list prices below the market price where you want your book sold. I provide more context to the pricing component in chapters 8 and 9 of this book.

Book Lending (Optional)

Allow your customers to lend your book to others

Terms & Conditions

Publish your Kindle eBook!

The fields for a Paperback book are:

Paperback Details

Language

Book Title

Subtitle (Optional)

Series, Series Name, and Series Number (Optional)

Edition Number (Optional)

Author Name: Primary Author or Contributor

Contributors (Optional)

(Editor, Foreword, Illustrator, Introduction, Narrator, Photographer, Preface, Translator, Contributions By)

Description

Up to 4000 characters. Take your time on this section. Other people will use this information to decide if they want to purchase your book or not.

Publishing Rights

Do you own the copyright or it is a public domain work?

Keywords (Optional)

The keywords help someone searching in Amazon; they are better able to locate your book. Again, I recommend getting help on this portion of the book because this can affect how others view your book. Fiverr is a great resource to use when selecting keywords for your book. You are allowed to input up to seven keywords.

Categories

(Fiction, Nonfiction, Juvenile Fiction, Juvenile Nonfiction, Comic and Graphic Novels, Education and Reference, Literary Collections, Non Classifiable) Within each category, there are multiple subcategories. You can select two categories.

Adult Content

Is this book appropriate for children under 18 years of age?

Paperback Content

Print ISBN

Get a free KDP ISBN or use my own ISBN

Publication Date (Optional)

Print Options

Interior and paper type: black and white with cream paper, black and white interior with white paper, premium color interior with white paper

Trim size: select the size of your book

Bleed settings: bleed or no bleed allows printing on or off the page

Paperback cover finish: matte or glossy

Manuscript

Upload your Paperback Manuscript

Book Preview

Paperback Rights and Pricing

Territories

All territories (worldwide rights) or Individual territories

Pricing & Royalty

I provide more context to the pricing component in chapters 8 and 9.

Terms & Conditions

Publish your Paperback Book!

I have good news for you! If you do not have all the information to fill in the appropriate fields, you can always go back and add it before you complete your book. Be sure to save the information you have already entered.

Once I selected my book size and entered the information into *KDP*, I decided which site I would use to format my book and prepare it for upload. To format my eBook, I downloaded Kindle Create from *Amazon KDP*. For my paperback book, I used Microsoft Word and utilized the *KDP* Build Your Book – Format a Paperback Manuscript document, located on the *Amazon KDP* site.

This paper document file (PDF) walks you through the process of formatting your entire book. Once you have completed the formatting steps, you will proceed more quickly through the remaining phases of publishing your book.

Chapter 3: Front Matter

Before editing your book, check that the key sections of the book are in place.

<u>*Personal Mistake story*****</u> When I was publishing my first book, I made the mistake of adding the front and back matter sections *after* I edited the book. My mistake required an additional edit afterward. Do not be like me - lol. Add your front and back matter *before* editing.

What is Front Matter?

Pages that appear at the front of a book, such as a title page and preface, are called Front Matter.

Front Matter material should include but is not limited to:

Title Page

Publisher Info

Copy Right Information

Dedication Page

Preface

Acknowledgements

Foreword

Table of Contents

Prologue

I used *Amazon KDP's* resources to create the front matter for my book, "*Things I Learned Before I Turned 31,*" including publisher information, table of contents, copyright information, and title pages. Be sure to place all the pages that make up your front matter in the correct order; review your writing resources to verify. I also added a dedication page, a preface, and a friend wrote my foreword.

Remember: Someone else is supposed to write the foreword for your book.

Helpful Tip: If you want a foreword, this is an excellent opportunity to ask a friend or family member for assistance. Include them in your project. You never know who would love to help and be a part of your book.

Chapter 4: Back Matter

What is Back Matter?

Back matter is the support material that goes at the back of a book such as appendices, notes, references, and glossaries.

Back matter material may include but is not limited to:

Acknowledgments

Bibliography

About the Author

Appendix

Author's Note

Conclusion

Glossary

Epilogue

In my book's back matter, I included my bibliography, the conclusion, about the author, and acknowledgments.

Remember, if you are quoting someone or utilizing content from other sources, you may need to ask those sources for permission. Remember as well, to cite your sources in your bibliography.

Your back matter depends on the type of book you want to publish. Go through the back matter components and determine which ones to include in your book.

Chapter 5: Editor Sites

I created my first book manuscript from a collection of my favorite blogs.

After reviewing my current blogs, I realized that I needed someone to proofread my book's existing content. My first step was to find an editor. I printed out my entire manuscript, double-spaced it, and re-read it looking for grammatical errors and correcting them.

A wise woman, named T. Hubbard, once told me that the best way to check for errors with a book is to read each sentence backward. After re-reading everything, I was ready to look for my editor.

Once again, I turned to Google for help. As a blogger, I needed someone experienced with blogs. Google referred me to Upwork and Reedsy, two great sites that enable you to customize your book's content according to your needs and preferences. You can see people's resumés and their education credentials and specialties. Both sites allowed me to customize my search utilizing keywords such as editor, blogger, proofreading, etc. Your content search may be different if you want to publish a recipe book, a fitness guide, autobiography, biography, non-fiction, or fiction book. Be sure to customize your search based on your content.

Finding an Editor

Next, I posted a request on both sites and reviewed the freelance workers' credentials and pricing. For my first book, I wanted to ensure that the editor did not change my blog's content from its original text and meaning but only proofread for clarity.

My search request to potential editors was something like this:

"I am looking for someone who has experience working with blogs to proofread them for errors and check my word usage. I also have a short turn around and need them back within 48 business hours."

I found someone on Upwork and hired the person. They were excellent and quick. They reviewed my content for punctuation and spacing and ensured my content was readable. I had three editors review my work to double-check for grammatical errors. I added the front matter late; that's why I utilized three different editors. I recommend having at least two editors to review your work. During my publishing phase, I hired one person. Then I re-read the book, made additional corrections, and then hired a second person. Afterward, I re-read my book a third time.

Editor Pricing – Flat Rate vs. Paying per Word

Before hiring an editor, the Upwork site lets you ask your potential editor questions through its messaging system. Editors' fees vary according to their qualifications and experience, *as well as the length and content of your book.* I found it easier and more affordable for my book to do a flat rate versus paying per word.

If you are using Microsoft Word to write your book, check the bottom of your monitor screen—while you have your book Word document open— to see its word and page counts. Your potential editors might want the information to assess how long it would take to edit your book.

Be sure to have conversations with several editors before making your selection. Think of finding an editor as an interview process to produce your best work product. This book is your book and a representation of you, so you want to be comfortable with the person you hire.

Ask the Editor Questions Prior to Hiring Them

Before hiring an editor, ask as many questions as you want, including asking for a quote for a flat rate fee versus paying per word. I used Upwork for my editor. The site allowed me to set a due date to hold my editor accountable for returning my edited manuscript to me on time.

Since my manuscript was less than 120 pages, I usually gave each editor 48 hours to review my book. Before you hire, feel free to discuss how long it will take your editor to edit your book. Every editor I hired exceeded my expectations and returned my book to me within a 24-hour time period.

Once you hire your editor, you decide if you want to pay them upfront, pay them in milestones, or pay them at the end of the assignment. When I wrote my book, I did a small payment milestone of $5.00, and then once they sent me the information back for review, I paid the remaining balance of our agreed-upon price.

What Should You Ask the Editor

Below are the questions I asked my editor. Feel free to ask additional questions. You can also customize your questions based on your manuscript.

Five Helpful Questions I Asked my Editor

1. Do you have experience reviewing content related to blogs?
2. How long will it take you to edit my manuscript?

3. Can you provide a quote for my book that is 104 pages based on my page count? If I wanted to do a flat fee rate, will you accept this amount?

4. How much of a pre-payment do you require prior to completion of the book?

5. Can you edit my blog content only without changing the context of the original text?

Publishing Tip: If you are publishing a paperback, I always create my table of contents (TOC) last. I am known for adding and removing things last minute, so I add the TOC after all editing actions are complete.

If you are publishing an eBook using Kindle Creates, I suggest not making a table of contents. Kindle Creates will create one for you once you upload your manuscript. Also, I do not upload my document to Kindle Creates until all editing on my book is complete.

Chapter 6: Marketing and Ads

Next, I began to work on my marketing strategy. You want to create a buzz around your book before its release.

Take time to clarify who the target audience is for your book. The following three questions will help guide you in doing so.

The Three Main Questions I Asked Myself Were:

1. Who is my audience?
2. How does my audience find out about new books?
3. How can I turn my readers into faithful fans?

As I already had a login for Upwork and Reedsy, I utilized their free and supportive content to self-publish my first book. The great thing about Reedsy is that they provide each of their subscribers with free content on self-publishing. I took all their free courses and learned how to self-publish and market my book.

As a self-published author, you will want others to purchase your book, read it, and then share it. Through trial and error, I learned that the best way to sell my book, as I wasn't a celebrity and did not have a mega platform, was through word of mouth and social media.

People who know and support you will buy from you. Strangers may purchase from you because of a recommendation from someone else or because they believe in you, your story, or your relatable content. Always be as authentic as possible.

E-Mail List

In addition to working on a marketing strategy, you MUST build an e-mail list.

*Personal Mistake story***** I will be honest; I did not have an e-mail list for my first book. However, after releasing the book, I started building a small subscription list, and I look forward to making it grow.

Create your subscription list with the contact information from your friends, family, your website and blog e-mail subscription list, including people who attended an event you hosted.

Another way to create a subscription list is by using sneak peeks of your book before its release.

Sneak peeks create awareness of your book on social media. Create a post on social media, saying that your book is due for release. Then create another post with a paragraph or two from the first chapter. Then do another post containing the first page with that chapter. Ask readers for their comments. Ask readers to send you their e-mail addresses through direct-message if they would like to read the rest of the chapter.

Advertisements

When I was releasing my book, I also purchased a few Facebook and Instagram advertisements. They ran for a couple of days to gain momentum around my book. You can pay from a couple of dollars to much more for an advertisement through Facebook or Instagram.

You can also purchase advertisements through *Amazon KDP*; however, I did not do so. *Amazon KDP* advertisements start at $100.00 minimum.

Chapter 7: Book Covers

While the book editing process is proceeding, you should work on your book cover. *Amazon KDP* provides free book cover templates for its clients. For my first book about my life experiences, I decided to complete a photo shoot. Your book cover will depend on the genre and content of your book. If you want to use your own book cover, be sure to follow the guidelines in the *KDP* free resource guide for uploading your image to *Amazon KDP*.

The *KDP* guide will walk you through all the steps of working on and formatting your book cover. For my first book, I created my book cover in Microsoft Publisher and uploaded it to the *KDP* site as a jpg.

 Because this book, entitled *"My Self-Publishing Secrets,"* is more of a how-to guide, I outsourced its book cover to someone via the Fiverr site. The person put together my book cover and the back of my book with a one-day turnaround. I will use this site again unless my picture is on the cover or someone else designs my cover.

Before agreeing to pay for something on a third party site, please be sure you know what you are paying for and if it will work for your book.

If you want to add a book title to your book's spine, be sure to read the *KDP* information to see if your book contains enough pages to qualify for a book-spine.

There are tons of little steps to navigate and perform when publishing a book. Once you see the final product, however, your many endeavors will be worth every single minute you spent working on your book.

Chapter 8: Pricing Your Book

When I published my paperback book last year, I had a price point. *Amazon KDP* suggested a price point for my eBook based on their analytics, which I accepted.

If you are unsure how to establish a price point for your book, conduct a survey poll among your friends, family, and social media followers, and ask them what they are willing to pay for a book. You can also check comparable book prices in size and genre on different websites. Ultimately, you decide your book price point, but do your research to ensure your book price is in a competitive range.

Amazon KDP has a price range of $2.99 - $9.99 for an eBook. *Amazon KDP* is flexible; it allows you to set your book price for a couple of weeks and see how well your book does. After a few weeks, *KDP* analyzes the sales and you determine if you should change your price point or not.

For your eBook, Amazon displays your price point in other markets around the world. After you select your primary market, your eBook becomes available for purchase in at least 12 additional markets.

Your paperback book will be available in another seven markets in addition to your primary market.

Chapter 9: Royalties

*A*mazon *KDP* has a couple of different options for your royalty payout percentage.

When you set up your book, you will have the option to opt-in your eBook for *KDP* Select Enrollment to maximize your earnings. If you activate the option, your royalty percentage will be much higher. However, this option only allows you to sell your eBook through *Amazon KDP* within the selected timeframe.

For my book, I decided to opt-in for *KDP* Select Enrollment to maximize my earnings even though I could only sell my book through Amazon.

The royalty percentages may vary if you publish an eBook or a paperback. *Amazon KDP* has a royalty calculator that allows you to play around with the royalty percentage and check your payout per book compared to the book's price. After making your selection, the royalty calculator will show you your estimated royalty payout throughout the rest of the publishing process.

Royalty Payouts

Amazon KDP pays royalties 60 days after the end of the month in which the sale was reported. The easiest way to describe this is with an example. My first book sale was on September 1, 2019. I received my first royalty check at the end of November 2019. The *Amazon KDP* site has a royalty calculator and contains in-depth royalty information and forums for all your questions.

Amazon also allows you to track your royalties earned as your book sales. Their site shows your royalties earned by the day, week, month, and year as you have more historical sales data to view.

Chapter 10: Publishing Your Book

You are finally in the last chapter of this book. You made it! The most crucial suggestion I can give to you before you click the submit button is to review all your pages one last time. Once you submit your document for approval, pay attention to your e-mail; Amazon may have-additional changes or recommendations for you to make before your book is published.

When I released my first book, *AmazonKDP* approved my eBook much more quickly than my paperback book. The issue was the formatted size of the paperback cover being off by about 0.034 inches. I called the *Amazon KDP* 1-800 number. A company representative walked me through the problem. And then boom! I received a thrilling e-mail saying that my book had been published!

Ordering Proof Copies

If you are publishing a paperback book, I have one last suggestion. Before you publish, order a proof copy from *KDP*. A proof copy is the best way to check for grammatical errors and to see how your book will look once published. I like to think of a proof copy as affording me a quality analysis of my book. I ordered one for my first book, and I will continue to use them for any future books I publish. After the publication of your paperback, you cannot go back and edit/correct certain fields. Ordering a proof copy is one foolproof way to double-check your book's quality before it goes to print.

If you publish an eBook using Kindle Create, you can also print a copy of your book before publication for review.

Once your book is approved, you become a published author! Make sure you celebrate this moment, as it is a huge accomplishment. Take a moment to soak up your achievement! I am so proud of you!

Tip: After publishing your book, have each of your friends and family purchase a copy and write a review. Positive review ratings attract other people to look at your book and stimulate sales.

Helpful Links

Amazon KDP: https://kdp.amazon.com/en_US/

Reedsy: https://reedsy.com/

Upwork: https://www.upwork.com/

Fiverr: https://www.fiverr.com/

My Website: www.wrenhowsway.com

Conclusion

Thank you for purchasing my book.

If you decide to go ahead and publish your book after reading mine, please be sure to let me know. I would love to have the opportunity to get to know you and to support you.

Also, leave me a review on Amazon. I cannot wait to read your comments and share the joy we experience in expressing ourselves through writing and publishing.

What is next for me? You can find out what I have planned by subscribing to my blog page at www.wrenhowsway.com and/or following me on Instagram: @_wrenhowsway.

Until then, keep writing, keep smiling, and stay safe and encouraged!

Bibliography

Dictionary.com, Dictionary.com, 2020.

"Kdp.amazon.com - Self Publishing | Amazon Kindle Direct ..." *Self-Publish EBooks and Paperbacks for Free with Kindle Direct Publishing, and Reach Millions of Readers on Amazon*, 2020, kdp.amazon.com/.

Acknowledgements

Wow! This is my second book and I am so grateful for an opportunity to share my writing gift with the world.

First off, thank you to God for allowing me to help bless someone else. I believe we are all helpers, one to another. I am happy to share my gift of teaching through this medium, writing books that others can read, learn, and share.

To my mother: thank you for raising me with strong Christian values, and for being a walking example of a woman of faith.

To my dad: may you continue to rest in peace.

To my siblings, Tish, Tiana, Catrina, Renisha, Rashun, Teija, Elizabeth and DJ: I am blessed to have you all in my life. I love you all.

To my friends: OMG, my boos and bruhs, thank you for supporting my crazy ideas and rocking with me. I thank God that he handpicked each one of you all to be part of my tribe. I love you all.

To all my readers: Thanks for trusting me and my knowledge as a writer to aid you in publishing your book. I appreciate you.

www.ingramcontent.com/pod-product-compliance
Lightning Source LLC
Chambersburg PA
CBHW061528250726
48657CB00005B/2135